The rehearsal. A comedy. As it is acted at the Theatres-Royal in Drury-Lane and Covent-Garden. By George, late Duke of Buckingham.

George Villiers

The rehearsal. A comedy. As it is acted at the Theatres-Royal in Drury-Lane and Covent-Garden. By George, late Duke of Buckingham.
Buckingham, George Villiers, Duke of
ESTCID: T046670
Reproduction from British Library
Possibly issued with 'Orpheus and Eurydice; an opera.' by Lewis Theobold.
London : printed for J. Wenman; and sold by all other booksellers in town and country, 1777.
19,[1]p., plate ; 8°

Gale ECCO Print Editions

Relive history with *Eighteenth Century Collections Online*, now available in print for the independent historian and collector. This series includes the most significant English-language and foreign-language works printed in Great Britain during the eighteenth century, and is organized in seven different subject areas including literature and language; medicine, science, and technology; and religion and philosophy. The collection also includes thousands of important works from the Americas.

The eighteenth century has been called "The Age of Enlightenment." It was a period of rapid advance in print culture and publishing, in world exploration, and in the rapid growth of science and technology – all of which had a profound impact on the political and cultural landscape. At the end of the century the American Revolution, French Revolution and Industrial Revolution, perhaps three of the most significant events in modern history, set in motion developments that eventually dominated world political, economic, and social life.

In a groundbreaking effort, Gale initiated a revolution of its own: digitization of epic proportions to preserve these invaluable works in the largest online archive of its kind. Contributions from major world libraries constitute over 175,000 original printed works. Scanned images of the actual pages, rather than transcriptions, recreate the works ***as they first appeared.***

Now for the first time, these high-quality digital scans of original works are available via print-on-demand, making them readily accessible to libraries, students, independent scholars, and readers of all ages.

For our initial release we have created seven robust collections to form one the world's most comprehensive catalogs of 18th century works.

Initial Gale ECCO Print Editions collections include:

History and Geography
Rich in titles on English life and social history, this collection spans the world as it was known to eighteenth-century historians and explorers. Titles include a wealth of travel accounts and diaries, histories of nations from throughout the world, and maps and charts of a world that was still being discovered. Students of the War of American Independence will find fascinating accounts from the British side of conflict.

Social Science

Delve into what it was like to live during the eighteenth century by reading the first-hand accounts of everyday people, including city dwellers and farmers, businessmen and bankers, artisans and merchants, artists and their patrons, politicians and their constituents. Original texts make the American, French, and Industrial revolutions vividly contemporary.

Medicine, Science and Technology

Medical theory and practice of the 1700s developed rapidly, as is evidenced by the extensive collection, which includes descriptions of diseases, their conditions, and treatments. Books on science and technology, agriculture, military technology, natural philosophy, even cookbooks, are all contained here.

Literature and Language

Western literary study flows out of eighteenth-century works by Alexander Pope, Daniel Defoe, Henry Fielding, Frances Burney, Denis Diderot, Johann Gottfried Herder, Johann Wolfgang von Goethe, and others. Experience the birth of the modern novel, or compare the development of language using dictionaries and grammar discourses.

Religion and Philosophy

The Age of Enlightenment profoundly enriched religious and philosophical understanding and continues to influence present-day thinking. Works collected here include masterpieces by David Hume, Immanuel Kant, and Jean-Jacques Rousseau, as well as religious sermons and moral debates on the issues of the day, such as the slave trade. The Age of Reason saw conflict between Protestantism and Catholicism transformed into one between faith and logic -- a debate that continues in the twenty-first century.

Law and Reference

This collection reveals the history of English common law and Empire law in a vastly changing world of British expansion. Dominating the legal field is the *Commentaries of the Law of England* by Sir William Blackstone, which first appeared in 1765. Reference works such as almanacs and catalogues continue to educate us by revealing the day-to-day workings of society.

Fine Arts

The eighteenth-century fascination with Greek and Roman antiquity followed the systematic excavation of the ruins at Pompeii and Herculaneum in southern Italy; and after 1750 a neoclassical style dominated all artistic fields. The titles here trace developments in mostly English-language works on painting, sculpture, architecture, music, theater, and other disciplines. Instructional works on musical instruments, catalogs of art objects, comic operas, and more are also included.

The BiblioLife Network

This project was made possible in part by the BiblioLife Network (BLN), a project aimed at addressing some of the huge challenges facing book preservationists around the world. The BLN includes libraries, library networks, archives, subject matter experts, online communities and library service providers. We believe every book ever published should be available as a high-quality print reproduction; printed on-demand anywhere in the world. This insures the ongoing accessibility of the content and helps generate sustainable revenue for the libraries and organizations that work to preserve these important materials.

The following book is in the "public domain" and represents an authentic reproduction of the text as printed by the original publisher. While we have attempted to accurately maintain the integrity of the original work, there are sometimes problems with the original work or the micro-film from which the books were digitized. This can result in minor errors in reproduction. Possible imperfections include missing and blurred pages, poor pictures, markings and other reproduction issues beyond our control. Because this work is culturally important, we have made it available as part of our commitment to protecting, preserving, and promoting the world's literature.

GUIDE TO FOLD-OUTS MAPS and OVERSIZED IMAGES

The book you are reading was digitized from microfilm captured over the past thirty to forty years. Years after the creation of the original microfilm, the book was converted to digital files and made available in an online database.

In an online database, page images do not need to conform to the size restrictions found in a printed book. When converting these images back into a printed bound book, the page sizes are standardized in ways that maintain the detail of the original. For large images, such as fold-out maps, the original page image is split into two or more pages

Guidelines used to determine how to split the page image follows:

- Some images are split vertically; large images require vertical and horizontal splits.
- For horizontal splits, the content is split left to right.
- For vertical splits, the content is split from top to bottom.
- For both vertical and horizontal splits, the image is processed from top left to bottom right.

THE

REHEARSAL.

A

COMEDY.

As it is Acted at the

THEATRES-ROYAL

IN

Drury-Lane and Covent-Garden.

By GEORGE, late DUKE OF BUCKINGHAM.

LONDON

inted for J. WENMAN, No 144, FLEET-STREET, and Sold by all other Booksellers in Town and Country

M DCC LXXVII

PROLOGUE.

AS when the merchant, to increase his store,
For dubious seas, advent'rous quits the shore;
Still anxious for his freight, he trembling sees
Rocks in each buoy, and tempests in each breeze,
The curling wave to mountain billows swells
And every cloud a fancied storm foretells
Thus rashly launch'd on this theatric main,
Our all on board, each phantom gives us pain,
The catcall's tune seems thunder in our ears,
And every hiss a hurricane appears,
In journal squibs the lightning's blasts espy,
And meteors blaze in every critic's eye
Spite of these terrors, still some hopes we view,
Hopes never can fail us—since they're plac'd—in you.
Your breath the gale, our voyage [illegible],
And safe the venture where your smiles insure,
Tho' weak his skill, the adventurer must succeed,
Where candour takes the lead and [illegible] for the deed
For Brentford's state, two kings could once suffice,
In ours, behold! four kings at Brentford rise,
All yielding to one mighty sov'reign's favour,
The sov'reign sway of the—publick favour
From hence alone, our royal fund we draw,
Your pleasure our support, your will our law.
While such our government, we hope you'll own us,
But should we ever grant prove—de-throne us
Like brother monarchs, who, to coax the nation,
Began their reigns, with some fair proclamation,
We too, should ask at least—of reformation,
Declare, that during our imperial sway,
No bard shall mourn his long-neglected play;
But then the play must have some wit, some sprite,
And we allow the umpire of its merit
For those deep sages of the judging pit,
Whose taste is too refin'd for modern wit,
From Rome's great theatre we'll cull the piece,
And plant, on Britain's stage, the flowers of Greece
If some there are our British bards can please,
Who taste the ancient wits, of ancient days,
Be ours to save, from time's devouring womb,
Their works, and snatch their laurels from the tomb
For you, ye fair, who sprightlier scenes may chuse,
Where music decks in all her airs the muse,
Gay opera shall all its charms dispense,
In [illegible] of tuneful triumph over sense,
The nobler bard shall still assert his [illegible],
Nor Handel rob a Shakespeare of his [illegible]
To [illegible] the [illegible] of our feasts,
[illegible] all the gods of pantomime shall rise
To boast the pomp and magic of machines,
Some pi[illegible] the [illegible]ing of our scenes
[illegible] good King R[illegible]'s day,
By [illegible], and last epilogue the play
If terms like these your suffrage can engage,
To fix our monarch's empire of the stage
Confirm our [illegible], your fair opinions,
And [illegible]

EPILOGUE.

THE play is at an end, [illegible]
Tho' circumstance [illegible] Bayes [illegible]
And [illegible] can boast, th[illegible]
[illegible] free from [illegible] the stage
Tho' ancients plotted, tho', and strove to please,
With sense that might be understood with ease,
They every scene with so much wit did store,
That who brought any in, went out with more.
But this new way of wit does so surprize,
Men lose their wits in wond'ring where it lies
If it be true, that monstrous births presage
The following mischiefs that afflict the age,
And sad disasters to the state proclaim,
Plays without head or tail may do the same
Wherefore, for ours, and for the kingdom's peace,
May this prodigious way of writing cease
Let's have at least once in our lives a time,
When we may hear some reason, not all rhime
We have these ten years felt its influence,
Pray let this prove a year of prose and sense

Dramatis Personæ.

MEN

Bayes
Johnson
Smith
Two Kings of Brentford.
Prince Prettyman
Prince Volscius
Gentleman-Usher.
Physician
Drawcansir
General.
Lieutenant General.
Cordelio
Tom Thimble.
Fisherman
Sun.
Thunder.
Players
Soldiers
Two Heralds
Four Cardinals, } Mutes.
Mayor, } Mutes.
Judges, } Mutes.
Serjeant at Arms, } Mutes.

WOMEN.

Amaryllis
Cloris
Parthenope
Pallas
Lightning
Moon
Earth

Attendants of Men and Women.

SCENE, BRENTFORD.

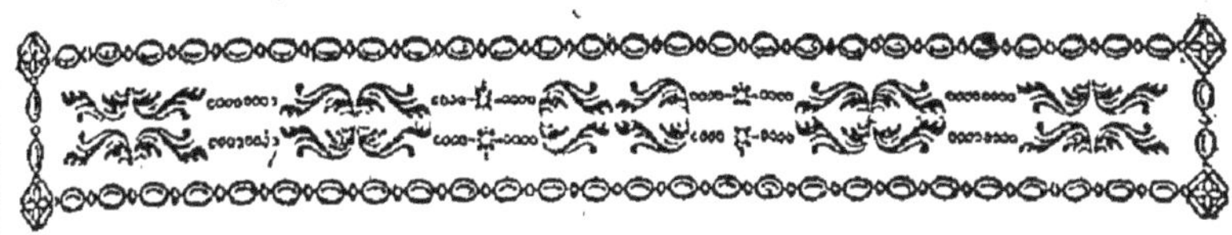

THE

REHEARSAL.

ACT I SCENE I

Johnson and *Smith*.

HONEST Frank, I am glad to see thee, with all my heart How long hast thou been in town?

Smith Faith not above an hour and if I had not met you here, I had gone to look you out, for I long to talk with you freely of all the strange new things we have heard in the country

Johns And, by my troth, I have long'd as much to laugh with you at all the impertinent, dull, fantastical things we are tired out with here

Smith Dull and fantastical! that's an excellent composition Pray what are our men of business doing?

Johns I never enquire after em Thou knowest my humour lies another way I love to please myself as much, and to trouble others as little as I can and therefore do naturally avoid the company of those solemn fops, who, being incapable of reason, and insensible of wit and pleasure, are always looking grave, and troubling one another, in hopes to be thought men of business.

Smith. Indeed I have ever observ'd, that your grave lookers are the dullest of men.

Johns Ay, and of birds and beasts too Your gravest bird is an owl, and your gravest beast is an ass

Smith Well, but how dost thou pass thy time?

Johns Why, as I used to do, eat, drink, as well as I can, have a she friend to be private with in the afternoon, and sometimes see a play, where there are such things, Frank, such hideous, monstrous things, that it has almost made me forswear the stage, and resolv'd to apply myself to the solid nonsense of your men of business, as the more ingenious pastime

Smith I have heard indeed you have had lately many new plays, and our country wits commend them

Johns Ay, so do some of our city wits too, but they are of the new kind of wits

Smith New kind! What kind is that?

Johns Why, your virtuosi, your civil persons, your drolls, fellows that scorn to imitate nature, but are given altogether to elevate and surprize

Smith Elevate and surprize! Prythee make me understand the meaning of that

Johns Nay, by my troth, that's a hard matter, I don't understand that myself 'Tis a phrase they have got amongst them, to express their no meaning by I'll tell you as near as I can what it is Let me see, 'tis fighting, loving, sleeping, rhyming, dying, dancing, singing, crying, and every thing but thinking and sense

Mr Bayes *passes over the stage*

Bayes Your most obsequious, and most observant, very servant, Sir

Johns God so, this is an author I'll go fetch him to you

Smith No, prythee let him alone

Johns Nay, by the Lord I'll have him

[*Goes after him*

Here he is, I have caught him Pray, Sir, now for my sake will you do a favour to this friend of mine?

Bayes Sir, it is not within my small capacity to do favours, but receive 'em, especially from a person that does wear the honourable title you are pleased to impose, Sir, upon this——Sweet Sir, your servant

Smith Your humble servant, Sir

Johns But wilt thou do me a favour now?

Bayes Ay, Sir What is t?

Johns Why, to tell him the meaning of thy last play

Bayes How, Sir, the meaning? Do you mean the plot?

Johns Ay, ay, any thing

Bayes Faith, Sir the intrigo's now quite out of my head, but I have a new one in my pocket, that I may say is a virgin, it has never yet been blown upon I must tell you one thing, 'tis all new wit, and, tho' I say it, a better than my last, and you know well enough how that took In fine, it shall read and write, and act, and plot, and shew, ay, and pit, box and gallery, i gad, with any play in Europe This morning is its last rehearsal, in their habits, and all that, as it is to be acted, and if you and your friend will do it but the honour to see it in its virgin attire, tho' perhaps it may blush, I shall not be asham'd to discover its nakedness unto you ——I think it is in this pocket

[*Puts his hand in his pocket*

Johns Sir, I confess I am not able to answer you in this new way, but if you please to [illegible], I shall be glad to follow you, and I hope my friend will do so too

Smith Sir, I have no business so considerable as should keep me from your company.

Bayes Yes, here it is No, cry you mercy, this is my book of Drama Common places, the mother of many other plays

Johns Drama Common places! Pray what's that?

Bayes Why, Sir, some certain helps that we men of art have found it convenient to make use of

Smith. How, Sir, helps for wit?

Bayes. Ay, Sir, that's my position; and I do here aver, that no man yet the sun e'er shone upon, has parts sufficient to furnish out a stage, except it were by the help of these my rules

Johns. What are those rules, I pray?

Bayes. Why, Sir, my first rule is the rule of transversion, or *regula duplex*, changing verse into prose, or prose into verse *alternative*, as you please

Smith. Well, but how is this done by rule, Sir?

Bayes. Why thus, Sir, nothing so easy, when understood, I take a book in my hand, either at home or elsewhere, for that's all one, if there be any wit in't, as there is no book but has some, I transverse it, that is, if it be prose, put it into verse, (but that takes up some time,) and if it be verse, put it into prose.

Johns. Methinks, Mr. Bayes, that putting verse into prose should be call'd transprosing

Bayes. By my troth, Sir, it is a very good notion, and hereafter it shall be so.

Smith. Well, Sir, and what d'ye do with it then?

Bayes. Make it my own. 'Tis so chang'd, that no man can know it. My next rule is the rule of record by way of table-book. Pray observe

Johns. We hear you, Sir. Go on

Bayes. As thus, I come into a coffee-house, or some other place where witty men resort, I make as if I minded nothing, (do ye mark?) but as soon as any one speaks, pop I slap it down, and make that too my own

Johns. But, Mr Bayes, are you not sometimes in danger of their making you restore, by force, what you have gotten thus by art?

Bayes. No, Sir, the world's unmindful, they never take notice of these things

Smith. But pray, Mr Bayes, among all your other rules, have you no one rule for invention?

Bayes. Yes, Sir, that's my third rule, that I have here in my pocket

Smith. What rule can that be, I wonder!

Bayes. Why, Sir, when I have any Thing to invent, I never trouble my head about it, as other men do, but presently turn over this book, and there I have, at one view, all that Persius, Montaigne, Seneca's tragedies, Horace, Juvenal, Claudian, Pliny, Plutarch's lives, and the rest, have ever thought upon the subject, and so, in a trice, by leaving out a few words, or putting in others of my own, the business is done

Johns. Indeed, Mr Bayes, this is as sure and compendious a way of wit as ever I heard of

Bayes. Sir, if you make the least scruples of the efficacy of these my rules, do but come to the Playhouse, and you shall judge of them by the effects

Smith. We'll follow you, Sir [*Exeunt*

Enter three Players upon the Stage.

1 Play. Have you your part perfect?

2 Play. Yes, I have it without book, but I do not understand how it is to be spoken

3 Play. And mine is such a one, as I can't guess for my life what humour I'm to be in, whether angry, melancholy, merry, or in love. I don't know what to make on't

1 Play. Phoo! the author will be here presently, and he'll tell us all. You must know this is the new way of writing, and these hard things please forty times better than the old plain way. For look you, Sir, the grand design upon the stage is to keep the auditors in suspence, for to guess presently at the plot, and the sense, tires them before the end of the first act. Now, here every line surprizes you, and brings in new matter; and then, for scenes, cloaths, and dances, we put quite down all that ever went before us, and those are things, you know, that are essential to a play

2 Play. Well, I am not of thy mind, but so it gets us money, 'tis no great matter.

Enter Bayes, Johnson, and Smith.

Bayes. Come, come in, Gentlemen, you're very welcome. Mr ---a---Ha' you your part ready?

1 Play. Yes, Sir

Bayes. But do you understand the true humour of it?

1 Play. Ay, Sir, pretty well

Bayes. And Amaryllis, how does she do? Does not her armour become her?

3 Play. O admirably!

Bayes. I'll tell you now a pretty conceit. What do you think I'll make 'em call her anon, in this Play?

Smith. What, I pray?

Bayes. Why, I make 'em call her Amaryllis, because of her Armour, ha, ha, ha!

Johns. That will be very well indeed

Bayes. Ay, it's a pretty little rogue, I knew her face would set off armour extremely, and, to tell you true, I writ that part only for her. You must know, she is my mistress

Johns. Then I know another thing, little Bayes, that thou hast had her, i'gad

Bayes. No, i'gad, not yet, but I'm sure I shall, for I have talk'd bawdy to her already

Johns. Hast thou, faith! Pr'ythee how was that?

Bayes. Why, Sir, there is in the French tongue a certain criticism, which, by the variation of the masculine adjective instead of the feminine, makes a quite different signification of the word, as, for example, *ma vie* is my life, but if before *vie* you put *mon* instead of *ma*, you make it bawdy.

Johns. Very true

Bayes. Now, Sir, I having observed this, set a trap for her the other day in the tyring-room. For this, said I, *adieu bel esperansa de ma vie*, (which, i'gad is very pretty) to which she answered, I vow, almost as prettily every jot, for said she, *Songes a ma vie, Monsieur*. Whereupon I presently snapp'd this upon her, *Non, non, Madam—Songes vous a mon*——by gad, and nam'd the thing directly to her

Smith. This is one of the richest stories, Mr Bayes, that ever I heard of.

Bayes. I, let me alone, i'gad, when I get to 'em, I'll nick 'em, I warrant you. But I'm a little nice, for you must know, at this time I am kept by another woman, in the city

Smith. How, kept! for what?

Bayes. Why, for a *beau garçon*. I am, i'fackins.

Smith. Nay, then we shall never have done

Bayes. And the rogue is so fond of me, Mr Johnson, that I vow to God I know not what to do with myself

Johns. Do with thyself! no, I wonder how thou can'st make a shift to hold out at this rate

Bayes. O devil! I can toil like a horse, only sometimes it makes me melancholy, and then I vow to gad, for a whole day together, I am not able to say you one good thing, if it were to save my life

Smith. That we do verily believe, Mr Bayes.

Bayes. And that's the only thing, i'gad, which mads me in my amours, for I'll tell you, as a friend, Mr Johnson, my acquaintance, I hear, begin to give out that I am dull. Now I am the farthest from it in the whole world, i'gad, but only, forsooth, they think I am so, because I can say nothing

Johns. Phoo, pox, that's all natur'dly done of 'em.

Bayes. Ay, gad, there's no trusting of these

tongues, but-------Come, let's sit down Look you, Sirs, the chief hinge of this play, upon which the whole plot moves and turns, and that causes the variety of all the several accidents, which you know are the things in nature that make up the grand refinement of a play, is, that I suppose two kings of the same place, as, for example, at Brentford, for I love to write familiarly Now the people having the same relations to 'em both, the same affections, the same duty, the same obedience, and all that, are divided amongst themselves in point of devoir and interest, how to behave themselves equally between 'em these kings differing sometimes in particular, tho in the main they agree, (I know not whether I make myself well understood)

Johns. I did not observe you, Sir Pray say that again

Bayes. Why, look you, Sir, (nay, I beseech you, be a little curious in taking notice of this, or else you'll never understand my notion of the thing,) the people being embarrass'd by their equal ties to both, and the sovereigns concerned in a reciprocal regard, as well to their own interest, as the good of the people, they make a certain kind of a------You understand me------Upon which there do arise several disputes, turmoils, heart-burnings, and all that------In fine, you'll understand it better when you see it

[Exit, *to call the Players.*

Smith. I find the author will be very much obliged to the players, if they can make any sense out of this

Enter Bayes

Bayes. Now, gentlemen, I would fain ask your opinion of one thing I have made a prologue and an epilogue, which may both serve for either, (that is, the prologue for the epilogue, or the epilogue for the prologue,) do you mark? Nay they may both serve too, i'gad, for any other play as well as this

Smith. Very well, that's indeed artificial.

Bayes. And I would fain ask your judgments, now, which of them would do best for the prologue for, you must know, there is, in nature, but two ways of making very good prologues The one is by civility, by insinuation, good language, and all that, to [illegible] in a manner, steal your plaudit from the courtesy of the auditors the other, by making use of some certain personal things, which may keep a hank upon such censuring persons, as cannot otherways, i'gad, in nature, be hinder'd from being too free with their tongues, to which end, my first prologue is, that I come out in a long black veil, and a great huge hangman behind me, with a furr'd cap, and his sword drawn, and there tell 'em plainly, That if out of good-nature they will not like my play, i'gad, I'll e'en kneel down, and he shall cut my head off Whereupon they all clapping---a --

Smith. Ay, but suppose they don't?

Bayes. Suppose! Sir, you may suppose what you please, I have nothing to do with your suppose, Sir, [illegible] at all mortified at it, not at all, Sir, I gad, [illegible] on it, Sir Suppose, quoth a!---Ha, ha, ha!

[*Walks away.*

Johns. Phoo! pr'ythee, Bayes, don't mind what he says, he's a fellow newly come out of the country, he knows nothing of what's the relish, here, of the town

Bayes. If I writ, Sir, to please the country, I should have followed the old plain way, but I write for some persons of quality, and peculiar friends of mine, that understand what flame and power in writing is, and they do me right, Sir, to approve of what I do

Johns. Ay, ay, they will clap, I warrant you, never fear it

Bayes. I'm sure the design's good, that cannot be deny'd And then for language, I gad, I defy 'em all in nature to mend it Besides, Sir, I have printed above a hundred sheets of paper, to insinuate the plot into the boxes, and, withal, have appointed two or three dozen of my friends to be ready in the pit, who, I'm sure, will clap, and so the rest, you know, must follow; and then, pray, Sir, what becomes of your suppose? Ha, ha, ha!

Johns. Nay, if the business be so well laid, it cannot miss

Bayes. I think so, Sir, and therefore would chuse this to be the prologue For if I could engage em to clap, before they see the play, you know it would be so much the better, because then they were engaged for, let a man write ever so well, there are now-a-days a sort of persons they call criticks, that, i'gad, have no more wit in them than so many hobby horses, but they'll laugh at you, Sir, and find fault, and censure things, that, i'gad, I'm sure they are not able to do themselves A sort of envious persons, that emulate the glories of persons of parts, and think to build their fame, by calumniating of persons that, i'gad, to my knowledge, of all persons in the world, are, in nature, the persons that do as much despise all that, as---a --In fine, I'll say no more of 'em

Johns. Nay, you have said enough of 'em, in all conscience, I'm sure, more than they'll e'er be able to answer

Bayes. Why, I'll tell you, Sir, sincerely and *bona fide*, were it not for the sake of some ingenious persons, and choice female spirits, that have a value for me, I would see 'em all hang'd, i'gad, before I would e'er set pen to paper, but let 'em live in ignorance like ingrates

Johns. I marry! that were a way to be reveng'd of 'em, indeed, and if I were in your place, now, I would do so.

Bayes. No, Sir, there are certain ties upon me, that I cannot be disengaged from, otherwise I would But pray, Sir, how do you like my hangman?

Smith. By my troth, Sir, I should like him very well

Bayes. But how do you like it, Sir? (for I see you can judge) Would you have it for a prologue, or the epilogue?

Johns. Faith, Sir, 'tis so good, let it e'en serve for both

Bayes. No, no, that won't do Besides, I have made another

Johns. What other, Sir?

Bayes. Why, Sir, my other is Thunder and Lightning.

Johns. That's greater, I'd rather stick to that

Bayes. Do you think so? I'll tell you, then, though there have been many witty Prologues written of late, yet, I think, you'll say, this is a *non pareil* I'm sure no-body has hit upon it yet For here, Sir, I make my Prologue to be a dialogue; and as, in my first, you see, I strive to oblige the auditors by civility, by good-nature, good language, and all that, so, in this, by the other way, *in terrorem*, I chuse for the persons Thunder and Lightning Do you apprehend the conceit?

Johns. Phoo, pox! then you have it cock sure They'll be hang'd before they'll dare affront an author that has 'em at that lock

Bayes. I have made, too, one of the most delicate, dainty similies, in the whole world, i'gad, if I know but how to apply it.

Smith. Let's hear it, I pray you

Bayes. 'Tis an allusion to love ——

So boar and sow, when any storm is nigh,
Snuff up, and smell it gathering in the sky,
Boar beckons sow to trot in chesnut-groves,
And there consummate their unfinish'd loves,
Pensive in mud they wallow all alone,
And snore and gruntle to each other's moan.

How do you like it now, ha?

Johns. Faith, 'tis extraordinary fine, and very applicable to Thunder and Lightning, methinks, because it speaks of a storm.

Bayes. I gad, and so it does, now I think on't. Mr. Johnson, I thank you, and I'll put it in *profeto.* Come out Thunder and Lightning.

Enter Thunder and Lightning.

Thun. I am the bold Thunder.

Bayes. Mr. Cartwright, prithee speak that a little louder, and with a hoarse voice. I am the bold Thunder. Pshaw! speak it me in a voice that thunders it out indeed. I am the bold Thunder.

Thun. I am the bold Thunder.

Light. The brisk Lightning I.

Bayes. Nay, but you must be quick and nimble. The brisk Lightning I. That's my meaning.

Thun. I am the bravest Hector of the sky.

Light. And I fair Helen, that made Hector die.

Thun. I strike men down.

Ligh. I fire the town.

Thun. Let critics take heed how they grumble,
For then I begin for to rumble.

Ligh. Let the ladies allow us their graces,
Or I'll blast all the paint on their faces,
And dry up their petre to soot.

Thun. Let the critics look to't.

Ligh. Let the ladies look to't.

Thun. For Thunder will do't.

Ligh. For Lightning will shoot.

Thun. I'll give you dash for dash.

Ligh. I'll give you flash for flash.
Gallants, I'll singe your feather.

Thun. I'll thunder you together.

Both. Look to't, look to't, we'll do't, we'll do't, Look to't, we'll do't. [*Twice or thrice repeated.*
[*Exeunt ambo.*

Bayes. There, no more. 'Tis but a flash of a Prologue: a droll.

Smith. Yes, 'tis short indeed, but very terrible.

Bayes. Ay, when the simile's in, it will do to a miracle, I gad. Come, come, begin the Play.

Enter first Player.

1 *Play.* Sir, Mr. Ivory is not come yet, but he'll be here presently, he's but two doors off.

Bayes. Come then, gentlemen, let's go out and take a pipe of tobacco. [*Exeunt.*

ACT II. SCENE I.

Bayes, Johnson, and Smith.

Bayes. NOW, Sir, because I'll do nothing here that ever was done before, instead of beginning with a scene that discovers something of the plot, I begin this Play with a whisper.

Smith. Umph! very new, indeed.

Bayes. Come, take your seats. Begin, Sirs.

Enter Gentleman Usher and Physician.

Phys. Sir, by your habit, I should guess you to be the Gentleman-Usher of this sumptuous place.

Ush. And by your gait and fashion, I should almost suspect you rule the healths of both our noble Kings, under the notion of Physician.

Phys. You hit my function right.

Ush. And you mine.

Phys. Then let's embrace.

Ush. Come.

Phys. Come.

Johns. Pray, Sir, who are those so very civil persons?

Bayes. Why, Sir, the Gentleman-Usher and Physician of the two Kings of Brentford.

Johns. But, pray then, how comes it to pass that they know one another no better?

Bayes. Phoo! that's for the better carrying on of the plot.

Johns. Very well.

Phys. Sir, to conclude.

Smith. What, before he begins?

Bayes. No, Sir, you must know they had been talking of this a pretty while without.

Smith. Where? in the tyring room?

Bayes. Why, ay, Sir. He's so dull! Come, speak again.

Phys. Sir, to conclude, the place you fill has more than amply exacted the talents of a wary pilot, and all these threatning storms, which, like impregnate clouds, hover o'er our heads, will (when they once are grasp'd but by the eye of reason) melt into fruitful showers of blessings on the people.

Bayes. Pray mark that allegory! Is not that good?

Johns. Yes! that grasping of a storm with the eye, is admirable.

Phys. But yet some rumours great are stirring; and if Lorenzo should prove false, (which none but the great gods can tell) you then perhaps would find that——— [*Whispers.*

Bayes. Now he whispers.

Ush. Alone, do you say?

Phys. No, attended with the noble— [*Whispers.*

Bayes. Again.

Ush. Who, he in grey?

Phys. Yes, and at the head of—— [*Whispers.*

Bayes. Pray mark.

Ush. Then, Sir, most certain 'twill in time appear,
These are the reasons that have mov'd him to't:
First, he——— [*Whispers.*

Bayes. Now the other whispers.

Ush. Secondly, they——— [*Whispers.*

Bayes. At it still.

Ush. Thirdly, and lastly, both he and they—— [*Whispers.*

Bayes. Now they both whisper. [*Exeunt whispering.*
Now, gentlemen, pray tell me true, and without flattery,
Is not this a very odd beginning of a Play?

Johns. In troth, I think it is, Sir. But why two Kings of the same place?

Bayes. Why, because it's new, and that's it I aim at. I despise your Johnson and Beaumont, that borrow'd all they writ from nature. I am for fetching it purely out of my own fancy, I.

Smith. But what think you of Sir John Suckling?

Bayes. By gad, I am a better poet than he.

Smith. Well, Sir, but pray why all this whispering?

Bayes. Why, Sir, (besides that it is new, as I told you before) because they are supposed to be politicians, and matters of state ought not to be divulged.

Smith. But then, Sir, why———

Bayes. Sir, if you'll but respite your curiosity till the end of the fifth act, you'll find it a piece of patience not ill recompensed. [*Goes to the door.*

Johns. How dost thou like this, Frank? Is it not just as I told thee?

Smith Why, I never did before this see any thing in nature, and all that, (as Mr Bayes says) so foolish, but I could give some guess at what mov'd the fop to do it But this, I confess, does go beyond my reach

Johns It is all alike, Mr Wintershull has inform'd me of this Play already And I'll tell thee, Frank, thou shalt not see one scene here worth o.. farthing, or like any thing thou canst imagine has ever been the practice of the world And then, when he comes to what he calls good language, it is, as I told thee, very fantastical, most abominably dull, and not one word to the purpose

Smith It does surprize me, I'm sure, very much

Johns Ay, but it won t do so long: By that time thou hast seen a play or two that I ll shew thee, thou wilt be pretty well acquainted with this new kind of foppery

Smith Pox on t, but there s no pleasure in him H s too gross a fool to be laugh d at

Enter Bayes

Johns I'll swear, Mr Bayes, you have done this scene most admirably, though, I must tell you, Sir, it is a very difficult matter to pen a whisper well.

Bayes Ay, gentlemen, when you come to write yourselves, on my word you ll find it so

Johns Have a care of what you say, Mr Bayes, for Mr Smith there, I assure you, has written a great many fine things already

Bayes Has he, i fackins? Why, then, I pray, S., how do you when you write?

Smith Faith, Sir, for the most part, I am in pretty good health

Bayes Ay, but I mean, what do you do when you write?

Smith I take pen, ink, and paper, and sit down

Bayes Now I write standing, that s one thing, and then another thing is, with what do you prepare yourself?

Smith Prepare myself! What the devil does the fool mean?

Bayes Why, I ll tell you now what I do If I am to write familiar things, as sonnets to Armida, and the like, I make use of stew'd prunes only, but when I have a grand design in hand, I ever take physic, and let blood For when you would have pure swiftness of thought, and fiery flights of fancy, you must have a care of the pensive part In fine, you must purge the belly

Smith By my troth, Sir, this is a most admirable receipt for writing.

Bayes Ay, 'tis my secret, and in good earnest, I think one of the best I have

Smith In good faith, Sir, and that may very well be

Bayes May be, Sir! I'gad, I'm sure on't *Experto crede Roberto* But I must give you this caution by the way, be sure you never take snuff when you write

Smith Why so, Sir?

Bayes Why, it spoil'd me once, i gad, one of the sparkishest plays in all England But a friend of mine at Gresham-College, has promis d to help me to some spirit of brains, and i gad that shall do my business

SCENE II

Enter the two Kings hand in hand

Bayes Oh, these are now the two Kings of Brentford, take notice of their stile, 'twas never yet upon the stage, but if you like it, I could make a shift perhaps, to shew you a whole Play, writ all just so.

1 King Did you observe their whispers, brother King?

2 King I did, and heard, besides a grave bird sing,
That they intend, sweetheart, to play us pranks

Bayes This is now familiar, because they are both persons of the same quality

Smith. 'Sdeath, this would make a man spew.

1 King If that design appears,
I'll lug them by the ears,
Until I make 'em crack

2 King And so will I, i'fack

1 King You must begin, *Ma foy*

2 King Sweet Sir, *pardonnez moy*

Bayes Mark that, I make em both speak French, to shew their breeding

Johns O, tis extraordinary fine!

2 King. Then spite of fate, we ll thus combined stand,
And, like two brothers, walk still hand in hand [*Exeunt Kings.*

Johns. This is a majestic scene, indeed

Bayes Ay, 'tis a crust, a lasting crust for your rogue critics, i gad, I would fain see the proudest of 'em all but dare to nibble at this, i gad, if they do, this shall rub their gums for 'em, I promise you It was I, you must know, that have written a whole Play just in this very same style, it was never acted yet

Johns How so?

Bayes I'gad, I can hardly tell you for laughing, (ha, ha, ha!) it is so pleasant a story, ha, ha, ha!

Smith What is t?

Bayes I gad the players refus d to act it Ha, ha, ha!

Smith That s impossible!

Bayes I'gad they did it, Sir, point-blank refus d it, i'gad ha, ha, ha!

Johns. Fie, that was rude

Bayes Rude! ay, i gad, they are the rudest, uncivillest persons, and all that, in the whole world, i'gad i gad, there s no living with em I have written, Mr Johnson, I do verily believe, a whole cart-load of things, every whit as good as this, and yet, I vow to g..., these insolent rascals have turn d em all back upon my hands again

Johns Strange fellows, indeed!

Smith. But pray, Mr Bayes, how came these two Kings to know of this whisper? For, as I remember, they were not present at it

Bayes No, but that s the actor s fault, and not mine, for the two kings shou'd (a pox take 'em) have popp d both their heads in at the door just as the others went off

Smith That, indeed, would have done it

Bayes Done it! ay, i gad these fellows are able to spoil the best things in Christendom I ll tell you, Mr Johnson, I vow to gad, I have been so highly disoblig d by the peremptoriness of these fellows, that I am resolv d hereafter to bend my thoughts wholly for the service of the nursery, and mump your proud players, i gad So, now Prince Prettyman comes in, and falls asleep, making love to his mistress, which, you know, was a grand intrigue in a late play, written by a very honest gentleman, a knight

SCENE III

Enter Prince Prettyman

Pret. How strange a captive am I grown of late!
Shall I accuse my love, or blame my fate?
My love I cannot, that is too divine,
And against fate what mortal dares repine?

Enter Chloris.

But here she comes.

Sure 'tis some blazing comet! Is it not?

[*Lies down.*

Bay. Blazing comet! Mark that, i gad, very fine

Pret. But I am so surpriz'd with sleep, I cannot speak the rest. [*Sleeps.*

Bayes. Does not that now, surprize you, to fall asleep in the nick? His spirits exhale with the heat of his passion, and all that, and swop he falls asleep, as you see. Now, here she must make a simile

Smith. Where's the necessity of that, Mr Bayes?

Bayes. Because she's surpriz'd. That's a general rule, you must ever make a simile when you are surpriz'd, 'tis the new way of writing

Cloris. As some tall pine, which we on Ætna find

T'have stood the rage of many a boist'rous wind,
Feeling without that flames within do play,
Which would consume his root and sap away;
He spreads his worsted arms unto the skies,
Silently grieves, all pale, repines, and dies:
So shrouded up, your bright eye disappears.
Break forth, bright scorching sun, and dry my
tears [*Exit.*

Johns. Mr Bayes, methinks this simile wants a little application, too

Bayes. No, faith, for it alludes to passion, to consuming, to dying, and all that, which you know, are the natural effects of an amour. But I'm afraid this scene has made you sad; for, I must confess, when I writ it, I wept myself

Smith. No truly, Sir, my spirits are almost exhal'd too, and I am likelier to fall asleep.

Prince Pretty-man starts up, and says ———

Pret. It is resolv'd [*Exit.*

Bayes. That's all

Smith. Mr Bayes, may one be so bold as to ask you one question now, and you not be angry?

Bayes. O Lord, Sir, you may ask me any thing what you please, I vow to gad, you do me a great deal of honour. You do not know me, if you say that, Sir

Smith. Then pray, Sir, what is it that this Prince here has resolv'd in his sleep?

Bayes. Why, I must confess, that question is well enough ask'd, for one that is not acquainted with this new way of writing. But you must know, Sir, that to out-do all my fellow-writers, whereas they keep their intrigo secret, till the very last scene before the dance, I now, Sir (do you mark me?)
———

Smith. Begin the play and end it, without ever opening the plot at all?

Bayes. I do so, that's the very plain truth on't, ha, ha, ha! I do, egad. If they cannot find it out themselves, e'en let 'em alone for Bayes, I warrant you. But here, now, is a scene of business. Pray observe it, for I dare say you'll think no unwise discourse this, nor ill argu'd. To tell you true, 'tis a discourse I over-heard once betwixt two grand, sober, governing persons

SCENE IV

Enter Gentleman-Usher and Physician.

Ush. Come, Sir, let's state the matter of fact, and lay our heads together

Phys. Right, lay our heads together. I love to be merry sometimes, but when a knotty point comes, I lay my head close to it, with a snuff box in my hand, and then I fegue it away, i'faith

Bayes. I do just so, i gad, always

Ush. The grand question is, whether they heard us whisper? which I divide thus

Phys. Yes, it must be divided so, indeed

Smith. That's very complaisant, I swear, Mr Bayes, to be of another man's opinion, before he knows what it is

Bayes. Nay, I bring in none here but well bred persons, I assure you

Ush. I divide the question into when they heard, what they heard, and whether they heard or no.

Johns. Most admirably divided, I swear!

Ush. As to the when, you say, just now, so that is answer'd. Then, as for what, why, that answers itself, for what could they hear, but what we talk'd of? So that, naturally, and of necessity, we come to the last question, *videlicet*, whether they heard or no

Smith. This is a very wise scene, Mr Bayes

Bayes. Ay, you have it right, they are both politicians

Ush. Pray then, to proceed in method, let me ask you that question

Phys. No, you'll answer better, pray let me ask it you

Ush. Your will must be a law.

Phys. Come then, what is't I must ask?

Smith. This politician, I perceive, Mr Bayes, has somewhat a short memory.

Bayes. Why, Sir, you must know, that t'other is the main politician, and this is but his pupil

Ush. You must ask me whether they heard us whisper

Phys. Well, I do so.

Ush. Say it, then

Smith. Hey day! here is the bravest work that ever I saw

Johns. This is mighty methodical

Bayes. Ay, Sir, that's the way, 'tis the way of art, there is no other way, i gad, in business.

Phys. Did they hear us whisper?

Ush. Why, truly, I can't tell, there's much to be said upon the word whisper. To whisper in Latin is *susurrare*, which is as much as to say, to speak softly, now, if they heard us speak softly, they heard us whisper, but then comes in the *quomodo*, the how, how did they hear us whisper? Why as to that, there are two ways, the one by chance or accident, the other on purpose, that is, with design to hear us whisper

Phys. Nay, if they heard us that way, I'll never give 'em physic more.

Ush. Nor I e'er more will walk abroad before 'em.

Bayes. Pray mark this, for a great deal depends upon it towards the latter end of the play.

Smith. I suppose that's the reason why you brought in this scene, Mr Bayes

Bayes. Partly, it was, Sir, but I confess, I was not unwilling, besides, to shew the world a pattern here, how men should talk of business.

Johns. You have done it exceeding well indeed.

Bayes. Yes, I think this will do.

Phys. Well, if they heard us whisper, they will turn us out, and nobody else will take us

Smith. Not for politicians, I dare answer for it

Phys. Let's then no more ourselves in vain bemoan.
We are not safe until we them unthrone.

Ush. 'Tis right
And since occasion now seems debonair,
I'll seize on this, and you shall take the
chair

[*They draw their swords, and sit in the two great chairs upon the stage*

Bayes. There's now an odd surprize, the whole state's turn'd quite topsy-turvy, without any pother or stir in the whole world, i gad.

Johns. A very silent change of government, truly, as ever I heard of

Bayes It is so And yet you shall see me bring em in agun, by and by, in as odd a way every jot

[*The usurpers march off, flourishing their swords*
Enter Shirly

Shirly Hey ho! hey ho! what a change is here! Hey day, hey day! I know not what to do, nor what to say! [*Exit*

Johns Mr Bayes, in my opinion, now, that gentleman might have said a little more upon this occasion

Bayes No, Sir, not at all, for I underwrit his part on purpose to set off the rest.

Johns Cry you mercy, Sir

Smith But pray, Sir, how came they to depose the kings so easily

Bayes Why, Sir, you must know, they long had a design to do it before, but never could put it in practice till now, and, to tell you true, that's one reason why I made em whisper so at first

Smith O, very well! now I am fully satisfy'd

Bayes And then, to shew you, Sir, it was not done so very easily neither, in the next scene you shall see some fighting

Smith O, oh! so then you make the struggle to be after the business is done

Bayes Ay

Smith O, I conceive you. that, I swear, is very natural

SCENE V.

Enter four Men at one Door, and four at another, with their Swords drawn

1 Sold Stand Who goes there?

2 Sold A friend

1 Sold What friend?

2 Sold A friend to the house

1 Sold Fall on. [*They all kill one another*
[*Music strikes*

Bayes Hold, hold! [*To the music. It ceases* Now here's an odd surprize, all these dead men you shall see rise up presently, at a certain note that I have made, in *effaut flat* and fall a dancing Do you hear, dead men? Remember your note in *effaut fla*.

Play on [*To the music*

Now, now, now!

[*The music plays his note, and the dead men rise, but cannot get in order.*

O, out, out! Did ever men spoil a good thing so? No figure, no ear, no time, no thing? Udzookers, you dance worse than the angels in Harry the Eighth, or the fat spirits in the Tempest, I gad

1 Sold Why, Sir, tis impossible to do any thing in time, to this tune

Bayes O lord, O lord! impossible! Why, gentlemen, if there be any faith in a person that's a Christian, I sat up two whole nights in composing this air, and adapting it for the business for, if you observe, there are two several designs in this tune it begins swift, and ends slow You talk of time, and time, you shall see me do t Look you now, here I am dead [*Lies down flat on his face* Now mark my note *effaut flat* Strike up music Now [*As he rises up hastily, he falls down again* Ah, gadzookers, I have broke my nose

Johns By my troth, Mr Bayes, this is a very unfortunate note of yours, in *effaut*

Bayes A plague of this damn'd stage, with your nails and your tenter-hooks, that a gentleman can't come to teach you to act, but he must break his nose, and his face, and the devil and all Pray, Sir, can you help me to a piece of wet brown paper

Smith No, indeed, Sir, I don't usually carry any about me

2 Sold Sir, I'll go get you some within presently.

Bayes Go, go, then, I'll follow you Pray dance out the dance, and I'll be with you in a moment Remember and dance like horsemen

[*Exit* Bayes.

Smith Like horsemen! What a plague can that be?

[*They dance the dance, but can make nothing of it*

1 Sold A devil! let's try this no longer, play my dance that Mr Bayes found fault with so

[*Dance and Exeunt.*

Smith What can this fool be doing all this while about his nose?

Johns Pr'ythee let s go see [*Exeunt.*

ACT III SCENE I.

Bayes, *with a Paper on his Nose, and the two Gentlemen.*

Bayes NOW, Sirs, this I do, because my fancy, in this play, is to end every act with a dance

Smith Faith that fancy is very good, but I should hardly have broke my nose for it, tho'.

Johns That fancy I suppose is new too

Bayes Sir, all my fancies are so I tread upon no man's heels, but make my flight upon my own wings, I assure you Now, here comes in a scene of sheer wit, without any mixture in the whole world, I gad, between Prince Prettyman and his taylor It might properly enough be called a prize of wit, for you shall see em come in one upon another snip snap, hit for hit, as fast as can be. First one speaks, then presently t other's upon him slap with a repartee, then he at him again, dash, with a new conceit, and so eternally, eternally, I gad, till they go quite off the stage

[*Goes to call the players.*

Smith What a plague does this fop mean, by his snip snap, hit for hit, and dash?

Johns Mean! why he never meant any thing in his life, what dost talk of meaning for?

Enter Bayes

Bayes Why don't you come in?

Enter Prince Prettyman *and* Tom Thimble.

This scene will make you die with laughing, if it be well acted, for it is as full of drollery as ever it can hold 'Tis like an orange stuff'd with cloves, as for conceit

Pret But pr'ythee, Tom Thimble, why wilt thou needs marry? If nine taylors make but one man, and one woman cannot be satisfied with nine men, what work art thou cutting here for thyself, I trow!

Bayes Good

Tom Why, an't please your highness, if I can't make up all the work I cut out, I shan t want journeymen enough to help me, I warrant you

Bayes Good again

Pret I am afraid thy journeymen, tho, Tom, won t work by the day, but by the night

Bayes Good still.

Thim However, if my wife sits but cross-legg'd, as I do, there will be no great danger Not half so much as when I trusted you, Sir, for your coronation-suit

Bayes Very good, i faith.

Pret Why the times then liv'd upon trust, it was the fashion You would not be out of time, at such a time as that, sure a taylor, you know, must never be out of fashion

Bayes Right.

Tom I'm sure, Sir, I made your cloaths in the court fashion, for you never paid me yet

Bayes. There's a bob for the court

Pr. Why, Tom, thou art a sharp rogue when thou art angry, I see thou pay'st me now, methinks.

Bayes There's pay upon pay! As good as ever was written, i gad

Tom Ay, Sir, in your own coin, you give me nothing but words

Bayes Admirable, before gad!

Pr. Well, Tom, I hope, shortly, I shall have another coin for thee for now the wars are coming on, I shall grow to be a man of metal

Bayes O, you did not do that half enough

Johns Methinks he does it admirably

Bayes Ay, pretty well, but he does not hit me in't He does not top his part

Tom That's the way to be stamp'd yourself, Sir I shall see you come home, like an angel for the king's evil, with a hole bor'd thro' you [*Exeunt*

Bayes Ha, there he has hit it up to the hilts, i gad! How do you like it now, gentlemen? Is not this pure wit?

Smith 'Tis snip-snap, Sir, as you say, but methinks not pleasant, nor to the purpose, for the play does not go on

Bayes Play does not go on! I don't know what you mean, why, is not this part of the play?

Smith Yes, but the plot stands still

Bayes. Plot stands still! Why, what a devil is a plot good for, but to bring in fine things?

Smith O, I did not know that before

Bayes No, I think you did not, nor many things more, that I am master of Now, Sir, i gad, this is the bane of all us writers, let us soar but ever so little above the common pitch, i gad, all's spoil'd, for the vulgar never understand it, they can never conceive you, Sir, the excellencies of these things

Johns 'Tis a sad fate, I must confess, but you write on still for all that

Bayes. Write on! Aye, i gad, I warrant you 'Tis not their talk shall stop me if they catch me at that lock, I'll give 'em leave to hang me As long as I know my things are good, what care I what they say?—What, are they gone without singing my last new song! 'Sbud, would it were in their bellies I'll tell you, Mr Johnson, if I have any skill in these matters, I vow to gad this song is peremptorily the best that ever yet was written, you must know it was made by Tom Thimble's first wife after she was dead

Smith How, Sir, after she was dead?

Bayes Aye, Sir, after she was dead Why, what have you to say to that?

Johns Say! Why nothing He were a devil that had any thing to say to that

Bayes Right

Smith How did she come to die, pray Sir?

Bayes Phoo, that's no matter, by a fall But here's the conceit, that upon his knowing she was kill'd by an accident, he supposes, with a sigh, that she died for love of him

Johns Ay, ay, that's well enough, let's hear it Mr Bayes

Bayes 'Tis to the tune of Farewel, fair Armida on seas, and in battles, in bullets, and all that

SONG

In swords, pikes, and bullets, 'tis safer to be,
Than in a strong castle, remoted from thee:
My death's bruise pray think you gave me, tho' a fall
Did give it me more, from the top of a wall
For then if the moat on her mud would first lay,
And after, before you my body convey,
The blue on my breast when you happen to see,
You'll say with a sigh, there's a true blue for me.

Ha, rogues! when I am merry, I write these things as fast as hops, i gad, for you must know, I am as pleasant a debauchee as ever you saw, I am, i'faith.

Smith But, Mr Bayes, how comes this song in here? for methinks there is no great occasion for it

Bayes Alack, Sir, you know nothing, you must ever interlard your plays with songs, ghosts and dances, if you mean to——a——

Johns Pit, box, and gallery, Mr Bayes

Bayes I gad, and you have nick'd it Hark you, Mr Johnson, you know I don't flatter, i gad you have a great deal of wit

Johns. O lord, Sir, you do me too much honour

Bayes, Nay, nay, come, come, Mr Johnson, i'faith this must not be said amongst us that have it, I know you have wit, by the judgment you make of this play, for that's the measure we go by, my play is my touchstone. When a man tells me such a one's a person of parts, Is he so? says I, what do I do, but bring him presently to see this play, if he likes it, I know what to think of him, if not, your most humble servant, Sir, I'll no more of him, upon my word, I thank you I am *clara voyant*, i gad Now here we go to our business.

SCENE II

Enter the two Usurpers Hand in Hand

Ush But what's become of Volscius the Great?
His presence has not grac'd our courts of late

Phys I fear some ill, from emulation sprung,
Has from us that illustrious hero wrung

Bayes Is not that majestical?

Smith Yes, but who a devil is that Volscius?

Bayes Why, that's a prince I make in love with Parthenope

Smith I thank you, Sir

Enter Cordelio

Cor My lieges, news from Volscius the Prince.

Ush His news is welcome, whatsoe'er it be.

Smith How, Sir, do you mean whether it be good or bad?

Bayes Nay, pray, Sir, have a little patience Gadzookers, you'll spoil all my play Why, Sir, 'tis impossible to answer every impertinent question you ask

Smith Cry you mercy, Sir

Cor His highness, Sirs, commanded me to tell you,
That the fair person whom you both do know,
Despairing of forgiveness for her fault,
In a deep sorrow, twice she did attempt
Upon her precious life, but, by the care
Of standers-by, prevented was

Smith S'heart, what stuff's here?

Cor. At last,
Volscius the Great this dire resolve embrac'd
His servants he into the country sent,
And he himself to Piccadilly went,
Where he's inform'd by letters that she's dead

Ush Dead! Is that possible? Dead!

Phys O ye gods!

Bayes There's a smart expression of a passion O ye gods! That's one of my bold strokes, i gad.

Smith Yes, but who's the fair person that's dead?

Bayes That you shall know anon, Sir

Smith Nay, if we know at all, 'tis well enough

Bayes. Perhaps you may find too, by and by, for all this, that she's not dead neither

Smith Marry, that's good news indeed I am glad of that with all my heart

Bayes Now here's the man brought in, that is suposed to have kill'd her [*A great shout within*

SCENE III

Enter Amaryllis, *with a Book in her Hand, and Attendants*

Ama What shout triumphant's that?

Enter a Soldier

Sold Shy maid, upon the river-brink, near Twickenham town, the false assassinate is taken

Ama Thanks to the powers above for this deliverance I hope,
It's slow beginning will portend
A forward exit to all *future* end

Bayes Pish, there you are out, to all *future* end! No, no, to all future *end*! You must lay the accent upon *end*, or else you lose the conceit

Smith I see you are very perfect in these matters

Bayes. Ay, Sir, I have been long enough at it, one would think, to know something

Enter Soldiers dragging in an old Fisherman

Ama Villain, what monster did corrupt thy mind
T'attack the noblest soul of human kind
Tell me who sets thee on?

Fish Prince Prettyman

Ama To kill whom?

Fish Prince Prettyman

Ama What, did Prince Prettyman hire you to kill Prince Prettyman?

Fish No, Prince Volscius.

Ama To kill whom?

Fish Prince Volscius

Ama What, did Prince Volscius hire you to kill Prince Volscius?

Fish No, Prince Prettyman

Ama So, drag him hence,
Till fortune of the rick produce his sense [*Exeunt*

Bayes Mark how I make the horror of his guilt confound his intellects, for he's out at one and t'other, and that's the design of this scene

Smith I see, Sir, you have a several design for every scene

Bayes Ay, that's my way of writing, and so, Sir, I can dispatch you a whole play, before another man, i gad, can make an end of his plot

SCENE IV

S[illegible] now enter Prince Prettyman in a rage Where the devil is he Why, Prettyman Why, when, I say? O fie, fie, fie, fie! all's marr'd, I vow to g[ad], quite marr'd

Enter Prettyman

Phoo, pox, you are come too late, Sir, now you m[ay] go out again if you please, I vow to gad, Mr ——— I would not give a button for my play, no[w] you have done this

Pret What, Sir!

Bayes What, Sir! 'life, Sir, you should have come out in choler, rouze upon the stage, just as the other went off Must a man be eternally telling you of these things?

Johns Sure this must be some very notable matter he's so angry at

Smith I am not of your opinion

Bayes Pish! Come, let's hear your part Sir

Pret Bring in my father Why d'ye keep him from me?
Altho a fisherman, he is my father
Was e'er son yet brought to this distress,
To be, for being a son, made fatherless?
And you just gods, rob me not of a father
The being of a son take from me rather. [*Ex.*

Smith Well, Ned, what think you now?

Johns A devil, this is worst of all! Mr Bayes, pray what's the meaning of this scene?

Bayes O cry you mercy, Sir I protest I had forgot to tell you Why, Sir, you must know that long before the beginning of this play, this prince was taken by a fisherman

Smith. How, Sir, taken prisoner?

Bayes Taken prisoner! O lord, what a question's there! Did ever any man ask such a question? Gadzookers, he has put the plot quite out of my head with this damn'd question! What was I going to say?

Johns Nay, the lord knows I cannot imagine

Bayes Stay, let me see, taken, O 'tis true Why, Sir, as I was going to say, his highness here, the Prince, was taken in a cradle by a fisherman, and brought up as his child

Smith Indeed!

Bayes Nay, prithee hold thy peace And so, Sir, this murder being committed by the river-side, the fisherman, upon suspicion, was seiz'd, and thereupon the prince grew angry

Smith So, so, now 'tis very plain

Johns But, Mr Bayes, is not this some disparagement to a prince, to pass for a fisherman's son? Have a care of that, I pray

Bayes No, no, not at all, for 'tis but for a while I shall fetch him off again presently, you shall see

Enter Prettyman *and* Thimble

Pret By all the gods, I'll set the world on fire,
Rather than let 'em ravish hence my sire

Thim Brave Prettyman, it is at length reveal'd,
That he is not thy sire who thee conceal'd.

Bayes Lo you now, there he's off again

Johns Admirably done, i'faith!

Bayes Ay, now the plot thickens very much upon us

Pret What oracle this darkness can evince!
Sometimes a fisher's son, sometimes a prince
It is a secret, great as is the world,
In which I, like the soul, am toss'd and hurl'd
The blackest ink of fate sure was my lot,
And when she writ my name, she made a blot
[*Exit*

Bayes There's a blustering verse for you now

Smith Yes, Sir, but why is he so mightily troubled to find he is not a fisherman's son?

Bayes Phoo! that is not because he has a mind to be his son, but for fear he should be thought to be nobody's son at all

Smith Nay, that would trouble a man indeed.

Bayes So, let me see

SCENE V

Enter Prince Volscius, *going out of Town*

Smith I thought he had been gone to Piccadilly

Bayes Yes, he gave it out so, but that was only to cover his design

Johns What design?

Bayes Why, to head the army, that lies conceal'd for him at Knightsbridge

Johns I see here's a great deal of plot, Mr. Bayes

Bayes Yes, now it begins to break, but we shall have a world of more business anon

Enter Prince Volscius, Chloris, Amaryllis, *and* Harry, *with a Riding cloak and Boots.*

Ama Sir, you are cruel thus to leave the town,
And to retire to country solitude

Chlo We hop'd this summer that we should at least
Have held the honour of your company.

Bayes. Held the honour of your company! Prettily express'd Held the honour of your company!

Gadzookers, these fellows will never take notice of any thing.

Johns. I assure you, Sir, I admire it extremely, I don't know what he does.

Bayes. Ay, ay, he's a little envious, but 'tis no great matter. Come.

Ama. Pray let us two this single boon obtain!
That you will here, with poor us, still remain!
Before your horses come, pronounce our fate,
For then, alas! I fear 'twill be too late.

Bayes. Sad!

Vols. Harry, Harry, my boots, for I'll go range among
My blades encamp'd, and quit this urban throng.

Smith. But pray, Mr Bayes, is not this a little difficult, that you were saying e'en now, to keep an army thus conceal'd in Knightsbridge?

Bayes. In Knightsbridge? Stay.

Johns. No, not if the inn-keepers be his friends.

Bayes. His friends! Ay, Sir, his intimate acquaintance, or else indeed I grant it could not be.

Smith. Yes, faith, so it might be very easy.

Bayes. Nay, if I do not make all things easy, egad I'll give you leave to hang me. Now you would think that he's going out of town, but you shall see how prettily I have contriv'd to stop him presently.

Smith. By my troth, Sir, you have so amaz'd me, that I know not what to think.

Enter Parthenope.

Vols. Bless me! how frail are all my best resolves!
How, in a moment, is my purpose chang'd!
Too soon I thought myself secure from love.
Fair Madam, give me leave to ask her name,
Who does so gently rob me of my fame:
For I should meet the army out of town,
And if I fail, must hazard my renown.

Par. My mother, Sir, sells ale by the town walls,
And me her dear Parthenope she calls.

Bayes. Now that's the Parthenope I told you of.

Johns. Ay, ay, egad you are very right.

Vols. Can vulgar vestments high-born beauty shroud?
Thou bring'st the morning pictur'd in a cloud.

Bayes. The morning pictur'd in a cloud! ah, gadzookers, what a conceit is there!

Par. Give you good even, Sir. [*Exit.*

Vols. O inauspicious stars! that I was born
To sudden love, and to more sudden scorn!

Ama. Clo. How, Prince Volscius in love! ha, ha, ha! [*Exeunt laughing.*

Smith. Sure, Mr Bayes, we have lost some jest here, that they laugh at so.

Bayes. Why, did you not observe? He first resolves to go out of town, and then, as he's pulling on his boots, falls in love with her. Ha, ha, ha!

Smith. Well, and where lies the jest of that?

Bayes. Ha! [*Turns to* Johnson.

Johns. Why, in the boots: where should the jest lie?

Bayes. Egad, you are in the right, it does lie in the boots——[*Turns to* Smith.] Your friend and I know where a good jest lies, tho' you don't, Sir.

Smith. Much good do't you, Sir.

Bayes. Here, now, Mr Johnson, you shall see a combat betwixt love and honour. An ancient author has made a whole play on't, but I have dispatch'd it all in this scene.

Volscius sits down to pull on his boots, Bayes stands by, and over-acts the part as he speaks it.

Vols. How has my passion made me Cupid's scoff!
This hasty boot is on, the other off,
And sullen lies, with amorous design,
To quit loud fame, and make that beauty mine.

Smith. Pr'ythee mark what pains Mr Bayes takes to act this speech himself!

Johns. Yes, the fool, I see, is mightily transported with it.

Vols. My legs, the emblem of my various thought,
Shew to what sad distraction I am brought.
Sometimes with stubborn honour, like this boot,
My mind is guarded, and resolv'd to do't,
Sometimes again, that very mind, by love
Disarm'd, like this other leg does prove.
Shall I to honour or to love give way?
Go on, cries honour; tender love says, Nay:
Honour aloud commands, Pluck both boots on;
But softer love does whisper, Put on none.
What shall I do? What conduct shall I find,
To lead me through this twilight of my mind?
For as bright day, with black approach of night
Contending, makes a doubtful puzzling light;
So does my honour, and my love together,
Puzzle me so, I can resolve for neither.
[*Goes out hopping, with one boot on, and the other off.*

Johns. By my troth, Sir, this is as difficult a combat as ever I saw, and as equal, for 'tis determined on neither side.

Bayes. Ay, is't not, now, egad, ha? For to go off hip hop, hip hop, upon this occasion, is a thousand times better than any conclusion in the world, egad.

Johns. Indeed, Mr Bayes, that hip hop, in this place, as you say, does a very great deal.

Bayes. O, all in all, Sir! they are these little things that mar, or set you off a play: as I remember once, in a play of mine, I set off a scene, egad, beyond expectation, only with a petticoat and the belly-ach.

Smith. Pray how was that, Sir?

Bayes. Why, Sir, I contriv'd a petticoat to be brought in upon a chair (no-body knew how) into a prince's chamber, whose father was not to see it, that came in by chance.

Johns. God's my life, that was a notable contrivance indeed.

Smith. Ay, but Mr Bayes, how could you contrive the belly-ach?

Bayes. The easiest i' th' world, egad, I'll tell you how. I made the prince sit down upon the petticoat, no more than so, and pretended to his father that he had just then got the belly-ach, whereupon his father went out to call a physician, and his man ran away with the petticoat.

Smith. Well, and what followed upon that?

Bayes. Nothing, no earthly thing, I vow to gad.

Johns. On my word, Mr Bayes, there you hit it.

Bayes. Yes, it gave a world of content. And then I paid 'em away besides, for I made them all talk bawdy, ha, ha, ha! beastly, downright bawdry upon the stage, egad, ha, ha, ha! but with an infinite deal of wit, that I must say.

Johns. That, ay, that, we know well enough, can never fail you.

Bayes. No, egad, can't it. Come, bring in the dance. [*Exit to call the Players.*

Smith. Now, the devil take thee for a silly, confident, unnatural, fulsome rogue.

Enter Bayes *and Players.*

Bayes. Pray dance well before these gentlemen: you are commonly so lazy, but you should be light and easy, tah, tah, tah.

[*All the while they dance, Bayes puts 'em out with being in the way.*

Well, gentlemen, you'll see this dance, if I am not deceiv'd, take very well upon the stage, when they are perfect in their motions, and all that

Smith I don't know how 'twill take, Sir, but I am sure you sweat hard for't

Bayes Ay, Sir, it costs me more pains and trouble to do these things, than almost the things are worth

Smith By my troth I think so, Sir

Bayes Not for the things themselves, for I could write you, Sir, forty of 'em in a day but, i gad, these players are such dull persons, that if a man be not by 'em upon every point, and at every turn, i gad, they'll mistake you, Sir, and spoil all

Enter a Player

What, is the funeral ready?

Play Yes, Sir

Bayes And is the lance fill'd with wine?

Play Sir, 'tis just now a doing

Bayes Stay then, I'll do it myself

Smith Come, let's go with him.

Bayes A match! But, Mr Johnson, i gad, I am not like other persons, they care not what becomes of their things, so they can but get money for 'em now, i gad, when I write, if it be not just as it should be in every circumstance, to every particular, i gad, I am no more able to endure it, I am not myself, I'm out of my wits, and all that I'm the strangest person in the whole world For what care I for money, I write for reputation

[*Exeunt.*

ACT IV SCENE I

Bayes, *and the two Gentlemen*

Bayes GEntlemen, because I would not have any two things alike in this Play, the last Act beginning with a witty scene of mirth, I make this to begin with a funeral

Smith And is that all your reason for it, Mr Bayes

Bayes No, Sir, I have a precedent for it besides, a person of honour, and a scholar, brought in his funeral just so and he was one (let me tell you) that knew as well what belong'd to a funeral, as any man in England, i gad

Johns Nay, if that be so, you are safe

Bayes I gad, but I have another device, a frolick which I think very better than all this, not for the plot or characters, (for in my heroick Plays, I make no difference as to those matters) but for another contrivance

Smith What is that, I pray?

Bayes Why I have design'd a conquest, that cannot possibly, i gad, be acted in less than a whole week And I'll speak a bold word, it shall drum, trumpet, shout, and battle, i gad, with any the most like tragedy we have, either ancient or modern

Johns Ay, marry, Sir, there you say something

Smith and pray, Sir, how have you order'd this same frolick of yours?

Bayes Faith, Sir, by the rule of romance, for example, they divide their things into three, four, five, six, seven, eight, or as many times as they please now I would very fain know what should hinder me from doing the same with my things, if I please

Johns Nay, if you should not be master of your own work, 'tis very hard

Bayes That is my sense And then, Sir, this contrivance of mine has something of the reason of a play in it too, for as every one makes you five acts to one play, what do I, but make five plays to one plot, by which means the auditors have every day a new thing

Johns Most admirably good, i faith! and must certainly take, because it is not tedious

Bayes Ah, Sir, I know that, there's the main point And then upon Saturday to make a close of all, (for I ever begin upon a Monday) I make you, Sir, a sixth play, that sums up the whole matter to 'em, and all that, for fear they should have forgot it

Johns That consideration, Mr. Bayes, indeed, I think will be very necessary

Smith And when comes in your share, pray, Sir?

Bayes The third week.

Johns I'll vow you'll get a world of money

Bayes Why faith a man must live, and if you don't thus pitch upon some new device, i'gad, you'll never do't, for this age (take it o'my word) is somewhat hard to please but there is one pretty odd passage in the last of these plays, which may be executed two several ways, wherein I'd have your opinion, gentlemen

Johns What is't, Sir?

Bayes Why, Sir, I make a male person to be in love with a female

Smith Do you mean that, Mr Bayes, for a new thing?

Bayes Yes, Sir, as I have order'd it You shall hear He having passionately lov'd her thro' my five whole plays, finding at last that she consents to his love, just after that his mother had appeared to him like a ghost, he kills himself That's one way The other is, that she coming at last to love him with as violent a passion as he lov'd her, she kills herself Now my question is, which of these two persons should suffer upon this occasion?

Johns By my troth, it is a very hard case to decide

Bayes The hardest in the world, i gad, and has puzzled this pate very much What say you, Mr Smith?

Smith Why truly, Mr Bayes, if it might stand with your justice now, I would spare 'em both

Bayes I gad, and I think—ha—why then, I'll make him hinder her from killing herself Ay, it shall be so Come, come, bring in the funeral

Enter a Funeral with the two Usurpers and Attendants.

Lay it down there, no, no, here, Sir So, now speak

K. Ush Set down the funeral pile, and let our grief
Receive from its embraces some relief

K. Phys Was't not unjust to ravish hence her breath
And, in life's stead, to leave us nought but death?
The world discovers now its emptiness,
And by her loss demonstrates we have less

Bayes Is not this good language now? Is not that elevate 'Tis my *non ultra*, i gad, you must know they were both in love with her

Smith With her! with whom?

Bayes Why this is Lardella's funeral

Smith Lardella! Ay, who is she?

Bayes Why, Sir, the sister of Drawcansir, a lady that was drown'd at sea, and had a wave for her winding-sheet

K. Ush Lardella, O Lardella! from above
Behold the tragic issues of our love
Pity us, sinking under grief and pain,
For thy being cast away upon the main.

Bayes Look you now, you see I told you true

Smith. Ay, Sir, and I thank you for it very kindly

Bayes. Ay, i'gad, but you will not have patience, honest Mr ——a—— you will not have patience

Johns Pray, Mr Bayes, who is that Drawcansir

Bayes Why, Sir, a fierce hero, that frights his mistress, snubs up kings, baffles armies, and does what he will, without regard to numbers, good manners, or justice

Johns A very pretty character

Smith. But Mr Bayes, I thought your heroes had ever been men of great humanity and justice

Bayes Ye, they have been so, but, for my part, I prefer that one quality of singl beating of whole armies, above all your moral virtues put together, i gad. You shall see him come in presently. Zookers, why don t you read the paper?

[*To the players*

K. Phys O, cry you mercy.

[*Goes to take the paper*

Bayes Pish! nay, you are such a fumbler. Come I'll read it myself [*Takes a paper from off the coffin*

Stay, it s an ill hand, I must use my spectacles This now is a copy of verses, which I make Lardella compose just as she is dying, with design to have it pinned upon her coffin, and so read by one of the usurpers, who is her cousin

Smith A very shrewd design that, upon my word, Mr Bayes.

Bayes And what do you think now, I fancy her to make love like, here, in this paper?

Smith Like a woman, what should she make love like?

Bayes O my word you are out tho, Sir, i gad you are.

Smith What then, like a man?

Bayes No, Sir, like a humble bee

Smith. I confess, that I should not have fancy'd

Bayes It may be so, Sir, but it is tho', in order to the opinion of some of your ancient philosophers, who held the transmigration of the soul

Smith Very fine

Bayes I ll read the title *To my dear Cousin*, King Phys

Smith. That s a little too familiar with a king tho, Sir, by your favour, for a humble-bee

Bayes Mr Smith, in other things, I grant your knowledge may be above mine, but as for poetry, give me leave to say, I understand that better, it has been longer my practice, it has indeed, Sir

Smith Your servant, Sir

Bayes Pray mark it [*Reads*

Since death my earthly part will thus remove,
I ll come a humble bee to your chaste love
With silent wings I ll follow you, dear coz,
Or else, before you, in the sun beams buz
And when to melancholy groves you come
An airy ghost, you ll know me by my hum,
For sound, being air, a ghost does well become.

Smith (*After a pause*) Admirable

Bayes At night, into your bosom I will creep,
And buz but softly, if you chance to sleep,
Yet in your dreams I will pass sweeping by,
And then both hum and buz before your eye

Johns By my troth that's a very great promise

Smith Yes, and a most extraordinary comfort to boot.

Bayes Your bed of love from dangers I will free,
But most from love of any future bee
And when with pity your heart-strings shall crack,
With empty arms I ll bear you on my back

Smith A pick-a-pack, a pick-a-pack

Bayes. Ay, i gad, but is not that tuant now ha? Is it not tuant? Here's the end

Then at your birth of immortality,
Like any winged archer hence I ll fly,
And teach you your first flutt'ring in the sky

Johns O rare! This is the most natural, refin'd fancy, that ever I heard, I ll swear

Bayes Yes, I think, for a dead person, it is a good way enough of making love, for being divested of her terrestial part, and all that, she is only capable of these little, pretty amorous designs, that are innocent, and yet passionate Come, draw your swords

K Phys Come, sword, come sheath thyself within this breast,
Which only in Lardella s tomb can rest

K. Ush. Come, dagger, come, and penetrate this heart,
Which cannot from Lardella s love depart

Enter Pallas.

Pal Hold, stop your murd ring hands
At Pallas s commands
For the supposed dead O kings!
Forbear to act such deadly things.
Lardella lives I did but try
If princes for their loves could die
Such celestial constancy
Shall by the gods rewarded be
And from these fun ral obsequies
A nuptial banquet shall arise

[*The coffin opens, and a banquet is discover'd.*

Bayes So, take away the coffin Now it's out This is the very funeral of the fair person which Volscius sent word was dead, and Pallas, you see, has turn d it into a banquet

Smith Well, but where is this banquet?

Bayes Nay, look you, Sir, we must first have a dance, for joy that Lardella is not dead. Pray, Sir, give me leave to bring in my things properly at least

Smith That, indeed, I had forgot I ask your pardon

Bayes O, d ye so, Sir? I am glad you will confess yourself once in an error, Mr Smith

DANCE.

K Ush Resplendent Pallas, we in thee do find
The fiercest beauty, and a fiercer mind
And since to thee Lardella s life we owe,
We ll supple statues in thy temple grow

K Phys Well, since alive Lardella's found,
Let in full bowls her health go round

[*The two Usurpers each of them take a bowl in their hands*

K Ush But where s the wine?

Pal That shall be mine
Lo, from this conquering lance
Does flow the purest wine of France

[*Fills the bowl out of her lance*

And to appease your hunger, I
Have in my helmet brought a pie
Lastly, to bear a part with these,
Behold a buckler made of cheese

[*Vanish Pallas*

Bayes There s the banquet Are you satisfy'd now, Sir?

Johns By my troth now, that is new, and more than I expected

Bayes Yes, I knew this would please you For the chief art in poetry is to elevate your expectation, and then bring you off some extraordinary way

Enter Drawcansir

K Phys What man is this that dares disturb our feast?

Draw. He that dares drink, and for that drink does die,
And knowing this, dares yet drink on, am I

Johns That is, Mr Bayes, as much as to say, that tho he would rather die than not drink, yet he would fain drink for all that too

Bayes Right, that's the conceit on't

Johns 'Tis a marvellous good one, I swear

Bayes Now, there are some criticks that have advised me to put out the second *dare*, and print *may* in the place on't, but, i'gad, I think 'tis better thus a great deal

Johns Whoo! a thousand times

Bayes Go on then

K Ush Sir, if you please, we should be glad to know,
How long you here will stay, how soon you'll go?

Bayes Is not that, now, like a well-bred person, i'gad?
So modest, so gent!

Smith O very like

Draw You shall not know how long I here will stay
But you shall know I'll take the bowls away

[*Snatches the bowls out of the Kings hands, and drinks 'em off*

Smith. But, Mr Bayes, is that, too, modest and gent?

Bayes No, i gad, Sir, but 'tis great.

K Ush Tho', brother, this grum stranger be a clown,
He'll leave us sure a little to gulp down

Draw Whoe'er to gulp one drop of this dare think,
I'll stare away his very power to drink

[*The two kings sneak off the stage with their attendants*

I drink, I huff, I strut, look big and stare,
And all this I do, because I dare [*Exit*

Smith I suppose, Mr Bayes, this is the fierce hero you spoke of?

Bayes Yes, but this is nothing You shall see him in the last act win above a dozen bottles, one after another, i gad, as fast as they can possibly come upon the stage

Johns That will be a sight worth the seeing, indeed

Smith But pray, Mr Bayes, why do you make the kings let him use 'em so scurvily

Bayes Phoo! that's to raise the character of Drawcansir

Johns O' my word, that was well thought on

Bayes Now, Sir, I'll shew you a scene indeed, or rather, indeed, a scene of scenes 'Tis an heroic

Smith And pray, Sir, what's your design in this scene?

Bayes Why, Sir, my design is gilded truncheons, forc'd conceit, smooth verse, and a rant, in fine, if this scene don't take, i'gad I'll write no more Come, come in, Mr ——a——ray, come in as many as you can Gentlemen, I must desire you to remove a little, for I must fill the stage

Smith Why fill the stage?

Bayes. O, Sir, because your heroic verse never sounds well but when the stage is full

SCENE II

Enter Prince Prettyman *and Prince* Volscius

Nay, hold, hold, pray by your leave a little Look you, Sir, the drift of this scene is somewhat more than ordinary, for I make 'em both fall out, because they are not in love with the same woman

Smith Not in love, you mean, I suppose, because they are in love, Mr Bayes?

Bayes No, Sir, I say not in love, there's a new conceit for you. Now speak.

Pret Since fate, Prince Volscius, now has found the way
For our so long'd-for meeting here this day,
Lend thy attention to my grand concern

Volf I gladly would that story from thee learn:
But thou to love dost, Prettyman, incline,
Yet love in thy breast is not love in mine.

Bayes Antithesis! thine and mine.

Pret Since love itself's the same, why should it be
Diff'ring in you from what it is in me?

Bayes Reasoning! i gad, I love reasoning in verse.

Volf Love takes, camelion like, a various dye,
From every plant on which itself does lie

Bayes Simile!

Pret Let not thy love the course of nature fright
Nature does most in harmony delight

Volf. How weak a deity would nature prove,
Contending with the pow'rful god of love!

Bayes There's a great verse!

Volf If incense thou wilt offer at the shrine
Of mighty love, burn it to none but mine
Her rosy lips eternal sweets exhale,
And her bright flames make all flames else look pale.

Bayes I gad that is right

Pret Perhaps dull incense may thy love suffice;
But mine must be ador'd with sacrifice.
All hearts turn ashes, which her eyes controul
The body they consume, as well as soul

Volf My love has yet a power more divine
Victims her altars burn not, but refine,
Amidst the flames they ne'er give up the ghost,
But with her looks, revive still as they roast
In spite of pain and death, they're kept alive,
Her fiery eyes makes 'em in fire survive

Bayes That is as well, i gad, as I can do

Volf Let my Parthenope at length prevail.

Bayes Civil, i'gad

Pret. I'll sooner have a passion for a whale,
In whose vast bulk, tho' store of oil doth lie,
We find more shape, more beauty in a fly

Smith That's uncivil, i gad

Bayes Yes, but 'tis far-fetch'd a fancy, tho, i gad, as e'er you saw

Volf Soft, Prettyman, let not thy vain pretence
Of perfect love, defame love's excellence
Parthenope is, sure, as far above
All other loves, as above all his love

Bayes Ah! i gad, that strikes me

Pret To blame my Chloris, gods would not pretend

Bayes Now mark

Volf Were all gods join'd, they could not hope to mend
My better choice For fair Parthenope
Gods would ungod themselves to see

Bayes Now the rant's a coming

Pret. Durst any of the gods be so uncivil,
I'd make that god subscribe himself a devil

Bayes Ay, gadzookers, that's well writ!

[*Scratching his head, his peruke falls off*

Volf Could'st thou that god from heaven to earth translate,
He could not fear to want a heav'nly state,
Parthenope, on earth, can heaven create

Pret Chloris does heaven itself so far excel,
She can transcend the joys of heaven in hell

Bayes There's a bold flight for you now! 'Sdeath, I have lost my peruke Well, gentlemen, this is what I never yet saw any one could write, but myself. Here's true spirit and flame all through, i'gad. So, so, pray, clear the stage.

[*He puts 'em off the stage.*

Johns. I wonder how the coxcomb has got the knack of writing smooth verse thus.

Smith. Why, there's no need of brains for this: 'Tis but scanning the labours on the finger; but where's the sense of it?

Johns. O; for that he desires to be excus'd: He is too proud a man to creep servilely after sense, I assure you. But pray, Mr. Bayes, why is this sense all in verse?

Bayes. O Sir, the subject is too great for prose.

Smith. Well said, i'faith; I'll give thee a pot of ale for that answer; 'tis well worth it.

Bayes. Come, with all my heart.
I'll make that god subscribe himself a devil!
That single line, i'gad, is worth all that my brother poets ever writ.
Let down the curtain. [*Exeunt.*

ACT V. SCENE I.

Bayes, *and the two Gentlemen.*

Bayes. NOW, gentlemen, I will be bold to say, I'll shew you the greatest scene that ever England saw: I mean not for words, for those I do not value; but for state, shew, and magnificence.——In fine, I'll justify it to be as grand to the eye every whit, i'gad, as that great scene in Harry the Eighth, and grander too, i'gad; for instead of two bishops, I bring in here four cardinals.

[*The curtain is drawn up, the two usurping Kings appear in state, with the four Cardinals, Prince* Prettyman, *Prince* Volscius, Amaryllis, Cloris, Parthenope, *&c. before them, Heralds and Serjeants at Arms, with Maces.*

Smith. Mr. Bayes, pray what is the reason that two of the cardinals are in hats, and the other in caps?

Bayes. Why, Sir, because—By gad I won't tell you. Your country friend, Sir, grows so troublesome——

K. Ush. Now, Sir, to the business of the day.

K. Phys. Speak, Volscius.

Vols. Dread sovereign lords, my zeal to you must not invade my duty to your son; let me intreat that great Prince Prettyman first to speak, whose high pre-eminence in all things that bear the name of good, may justly claim that privilege.

Bayes. Here it begins to unfold; you may perceive, now, that he is his son.

Johns. Yes, Sir, and we are very much beholden to you for that discovery.

Pret. Royal father, upon my knees I beg,
That the illustrious Volscius first be heard.

Vols. That preference is only due to Amaryllis, Sir.

Bayes. I'll make her speak very well, by and by, you shall see.

Amar. Invincible sovereigns—— [*Soft music.*

K. Ush. But stay, what sound is this invades our ears?

K. Phys. Sure 'tis the musick of the moving spheres.

Pret. Behold, with wonder, yonder comes from far
A god-like cloud, and a triumphant car,
In which our two right kings sit one by one,
With virgins vests, and laurel garlands on.

K. Ush. Then, brother, Phys. 'tis time we should be gone.

[*The two Usurpers steal out of the Throne, and go away.*

Bayes. Look you now, did not I tell you that this would be as easy a change as the other?

Smith. Yes, faith, you did so, tho' I confess I could not believe you; but you have brought it about, I see.

[*The two right Kings of* Brentford, *descend in the clouds, singing, in white garments, and three fiddlers sitting before them, in green.*

Bayes. Now, because the two right Kings descend from above, I make 'em sing to the tune and style of our modern spirits.

1 King. Haste, brother King, we are sent from above.

2 King. Let us move, let us move,
Move to remove the fate
Of Brentford's long united state.

1 King. Tarra, tan, tarra, full East and by South.

2 King. We sail with thunder in our mouth,
In scorching noon-day, whilst the traveller stays,
Busy, busy, busy, busy, we bustle along,
Mounted upon warm Phœbus's rays,
Thro' the heavenly throng,
Haling to those
Who will feast us at night with a pig's petty toes.

1 King. And we'll fall with our plate
In an olio of hate.

2 King. But now supper's done, the servitors try,
Like soldiers, to storm a whole half-moon pye.

1 King. They gather, they gather hot custards in spoons.
But, alas! I must leave these half moons,
And repair to my trusty dragoons.

2 King. O stay, for you need not as yet go astray;
The tide, like a friend, has brought ships in our way,
And on their high ropes we will play;
Like maggots in filberds we'll snug in our shell,
We'll frisk in our shell,
We'll frisk in our shell,
And farewel.

1 King. But the ladies have all inclination to dance,
And the green frogs croak out a coranto of France.

Bayes. Is not that pretty now? The fiddlers are all in green.

Smith. Ay, but they play no coranto.

Johns. No, but they play a tune that's a great deal better.

Bayes. No coranto, quoth ha! That's a good one, with all my heart. Come, sing on.

2 King. Now mortals that hear
How we tilt and career,
With wonder will fear
The event of such things as shall never appear.

1 King. Stay you to fulfil what the gods have decreed.

2 King. Then call me to help you, if there shall be need.

1 King. So firmly resolv'd is a true Brentford king,
To save the distressed, and help 'em to bring,
That ere a full pot of good ale you can swallow,
He's here with a whoop, and gone with a holla.

[Bayes *fillips his finger, and sings after 'em.*

Bayes. He's here with a whoop, and gone with a holla. This, Sir, you must know, I thought once to have brought in with a conjuror.

Johns. Ay, that would have been better.

Bayes. No, faith, not when you consider it; for thus it is more compendious, and does the thing every whit as well.

Smith. Thing! What thing?

Bayes Why, bring em down again into the throne, Sir, what thing would you have?

Smith Well, but methinks the sense of this song is not very plain

Bayes Plain! Why, did you ever hear any people in clouds speak plain? They must be all for flight of fancy at its full range, without the least check or controul upon it When once you tie up spirits and people in clouds, to speak plain, you spoil all

Smith Bless me, what a monster's this!

[*The two* Kings *alight out of the clouds, and step into the throne*

1 King Come, now to serious counsel we'll advance

2 King I do agree, but first, let's have a dance

Bayes Right, you did that very well, Mr Cartwright. But first, let's have a dance Pray remember that, be sure you do it always just so, for it must be done as if it were the effect of thought and premeditation But first, let's have a dance Pray remember that

Smith Well, I can hold no longer, I must gag this rogue, there's no enduring of him

Johns No, pr'ythee, make use of thy patience a little longer, let's see the end of him now

[*Dance a grand dance*

Bayes This, now, is an ancient dance, of right belonging to the Kings of Brentford, but since derived, with a little alteration, to the Inns of Court.

An alarm *Enter two* Heralds

1 King What saucy groom molests our privacies?

1 Her The army's at the door, and in disguise,
Desires a word with both you majesties

2 Her Having from Knightsbridge hither march'd by stealth.

2 King Bid em attend a-while, and drink our health

Smith How, Mr Bayes, the army in disguise!

Bayes Ay, Sir, for fear the usurpers might discover them that went out but just now

Smith Why, what if they had discovered them?

Bayes Why, then they had broke the design

1 King Here, take five guineas for those warlike men

2 King And here's five more, that makes the sum just ten

1 Her We have not seen so much the Lord knows when [*Exeunt* Heralds

1 King Speak on, brave Amaryllis

Ama Invincible sovereigns, blame not my modesty, if at this grand conjuncture———

[*Drums beat behind the stage*

1 King What dreadful noise is this that comes and goes?

Enter a Soldier *with his sword drawn*

Sol Haste hence, great Sirs, your royal person save,
For the event of war no mortal knows
The army, wrangling for the gold you gave,
First fell to words, and then to handy blows

[*Exit*

Bayes Is not that now a pretty kind of a stanza, [illegible] come off?

[illegible] O dangerous estate of sovereign power?
[illegible] to the change of every hour
[illegible] shelter in our cabinet [illegible]
[illegible] these threatning storms may pass [illegible]

[*Exeunt*

[illegible] Pray, Mr Bayes, did not you promise us [illegible] Amaryllis speak [illegible]? [illegible] so sh[illegible] [illegible], but what [illegible]

Smith How, Sir, whether you would or no?

Bayes Ay, Sir, the plot lay so, that I vow to gad it was not to be avoided

Smith Marry that was hard.

Johns But pray, who hindered her?

Bayes Why, the battle, Sir, that's just coming in at the door, and I'll tell you now a strange thing, though I don't pretend to do more than other men, i'gad I'll give you both a whole week to guess how I'll represent this battle

Smith I had rather be bound to fight your battle, I assure you, Sir

Bayes Whoo! there's it now fight a battle! there's the common error I knew presently where I should have you Why, pray Sir, do but tell me this one thing Can you think it a decent thing in a battle before ladies, to have men run their swords through one another, and all that?

Johns No, faith, 'tis not civil

Bayes Right, on the other side, to have a long relation of squadrons here, and squadrons there, what is it but dull prolixity?

Johns Excellently reason'd, by my troth!

Bayes Wherefore, Sir, to avoid both these indecorums, I sum up the whole battle in the representation of two persons only, no more, and yet so lively, that, I vow to gad, you would swear ten thousand men were at it really engag'd. Do you mark me?

Smith Yes, Sir, but I think I should hardly swear, though, for all that

Bayes By my troth, Sir, but you would though, when you see it For I make them both come out in armour, *cap-a-pie*, with their swords drawn, and hung with a scarlet ribbon at their wrist, which, you know, represents fighting enough

Johns Ay, ay, so much, that if I were in your place, I would make em go out again, without ever speaking one word

Bayes No, there you are out, for I make each of em hold a lute in his hand

Smith How, Sir, instead of a buckler?

Bayes O Lord O Lord! instead of a buckler? Pray, Sir, do you ask no more questions I make em, Sirs, play the battle *in recitativo* And here's the conceit Just at the very same instant that one sings, the other, Sir, recovers you his sword, and puts himself into a warlike posture, so that you have at once your ear entertained with music and good language, and your eye satisfied with the garb and accoutrements of war

Smith I confess, Sir, you stupify me

Bayes You shall see

Johns But, Mr Bayes, might not we have a little fighting? For I love those plays where they cut and slash one another upon the stage for a whole hour together

Bayes Why, then, to tell you true, I have contrived it both ways, but you shall have my *recitativo* first

Johns Ay, now you are right, there is nothing then can be objected against it

Bayes True, and so i'gad I'll make it to a tragedy in a trice

Enter [illegible] *the* General *and* Lieutenant-General, *arm'd* [illegible], *with each of them a* [illegible] *in his hand, and a sword drawn, and hung* [illegible]

Lieut Gen Villain, thou lie[illegible]!

Gen Arm, arm, Gonsalvo, arm, what ho!
The lie no flesh can brook, I trow.

Lieu Gen Advance from Acton with the musquetiers.

Gen. Draw down the Chelsea curassiers

Lieu. Gen. The band you boast of Chelsea curassiers,

Shall, in my Putney pikes, now meet their peers

Gen. Chiswickians, aged and renown'd in fight,
Join with the Hammersmith brigade

Lieut. Gen. You'll find my Mortlake boys will do them right,
Unless by Fulham numbers overlaid

Gen. Let the left wing of Twickenham foot advance,
And line that eastern hedge.

Lieu. Gen. The horse I rais'd in Petty-France,
Shall try their chance,
And scour the meadows, over-grown with sedge

Gen. Stand, give the word

Lieut. Gen. Bright sword

Gen. That may be thine,
But 'tis not mine

Lieut. Gen. Give fire, give fire at once give fire,
And let those recreant troops perceive mine ire

Gen. Pursue, pursue, they fly
That first did give the lie [*Exeunt*

Bayes This now is not improper, I think, because the spectators know all these towns, and may easily conceive them to be within the dominions of the two Kings of Brentford

Johns Most exceeding well design'd!

Bayes How do you think I have contriv'd to give a stop to this battle?

Smith How?

Bayes By an eclipse, which, let me tell you, is a kind of fancy that was yet never so much as thought of, but by myself, and one person more, that shall be nameless

Enter Lieutenant General

Lieut Gen. What midnight darkness does invade the day,
And snatch the victor from his conquer'd prey?
Is the sun weary of this bloody fight,
And winks upon us with the eye of light!
'Tis an eclipse! This was unkind, O moon,
To clap between me and the sun so soon
Foolish eclipse! thou this in vain hast done,
My brighter honour had eclips'd the sun,
But now behold eclipses two in one. [*Exit*

Johns This is an admirable representation of a battle, as ever I saw

Bayes Ay, Sir But how would you fancy now to represent an eclipse

Smith Why, that's to be suppos'd

Bayes Suppos'd! ay, you are ever at your suppose, ha, ha, ha! Why, you may as well suppose the whole play No, it must come in upon the stage, that's certain but in some old way that may delight, amuse, and all that I have a concept for't, that I am sure is new, and I believe to the purpose

Johns How's that?

Bayes Why, the truth is, I took the first hint of this out of a dialogue between Phœbus and Aurora, in the Slighted Maid, which, by my troth, was very pretty, but I think you'd confess this a little better

Johns No doubt on't, Mr Bayes, a great deal better

[*Bayes hugs Johnson, then turns to Smith*

Bayes Ah, dear rogue! But——a——Sir, you have heard I suppose, that your eclipse of the moon is nothing else but an interposition of the earth between the sun and moon, as likewise your eclipse of the sun is caused by an interlocation of the moon betwixt the earth and the sun

Smith I have heard some such thing indeed.

Bayes Well, Sir, then what do I, but make the earth, sun and moon, come out upon the stage, and dance the Hay Hum! and of necessity, by the very nature of this dance, the earth must be sometimes between the sun and the moon, and the moon between the earth and sun: And there you have both eclipses by demonstration

Johns That must needs be very fine, truly

Bayes Yes, it has fancy in't And then, Sir, that there may be something in't too of a joke, I bring 'em in all singing, and make the moon sell the earth a bargain Come, come out, Eclipse, to the tune of Tom Tyler.

Enter Luna.

Luna Orbis, O Orbis!
Come to me, thou little rogue, Orbis

Enter the Earth

Orb. Who calls Terra firma, pray?

Luna Luna, that ne'er shines by day.

Orb What means Luna in a veil?

Luna Luna means to shew her tail

Bayes There's the bargain

Enter Sol, *to the tune of* Robin Hood

Sol Fye, sister, fye! thou mak'st me muse,
Derry down, derry down,
To see thee Orb abuse

Luna I hope his anger 'twill not move,
Since I shew'd it out of love,
Hey down, derry down.

Orb Where shall I thy true love know,
Thou pretty, pretty moon?

Luna To-morrow soon, e'er it be noon,
On Mount Vesuvio

Sol Then I will shine
[*To the tune of* Trenchmore Bis.

Orb And I will be fine

Luna And I will drink nothing but Lippari wine

Omnes And we, &c

[*As they dance the Hay,* Bayes *speaks*

Bayes Now the earth's before the moon, now the moon's before the sun There's the eclipse again

Smith He's mightily taken with this, I see

Johns Ay, 'tis so extraordinary, how can he chuse?

Bayes So now, vanish eclipse, and enter t'other battle, and fight Here now, if I am not mistaken, you will see fighting enough

[*A battle is fought between foot and great hobby horses At last* Drawcansir *comes in, and kills 'em all on both sides All the while the battle is fighting,* Bayes *is telling them when to shout, and shouts with them*

Draw. Others may boast a single man to kill
But I the blood of thousands daily spill
Let petty kings the names of parties know
Where-e'er I come, I slay both friend and foe
The swiftest horsemen my swift rage controuls,
And from their bodies drives their trembling souls.
If they had wings, and to the gods could fly,
I would pursue, and beat them thro' the sky,
And make proud Jove, with all his thunder, see
This single arm more dreadful is than he [*Exit*

Bayes There's a brave fellow for you now, Sirs You may talk of your Hectors and Achilles, and I know not who, but I defy all your histories, and your romances too, to shew me one such conqueror as this Drawcansir

Johns I swear, I think you may

Smith But, Mr Bayes, how shall all these dead men go off? for I see none alive to help 'em

Bayes Go off, why, as they came on upon their legs how ſhould they go off? Why, do you think the people here don't know they are not dead? He's mighty ignorant, poor man! Your friend here is very ſilly, Mr Johnſon, i gad is he, Ha, ha, ha! Come, Sir, I'll ſhew you how they ſhall go off Riſe, riſe, Sirs, and go about your buſineſs There's go off for you now Ha, ha, ha! Mr Ivory, a word. Gentlemen, I'll be with you preſently [*Exit*

Johnſ Will you ſo? Then we'll be gone

Smith Ay, pr'ythee let's go, that we may preſerve our hearing One battle more will take mine quite away [*Exeunt*

Enter Bayes *and Players*

Bayes Where are the gentlemen?

1 Play They are gone, Sir

Bayes Gone! 'Sdeath! this act is beſt of all! I'll go fetch 'em again [*Exit*

1 Play What ſhall we do, now he's gone away?

2 Play Why ſo much the better, then let's go to dinner

3 Play Stay, here's a foul piece of paper Let's ſee what 'tis

3 or 4 Play Ay, ay, come, let's hear it

[*Reads* *The Argument of the Fifth Act*

3 Play Chloris at length, being ſenſible of Prince Prettyman's paſſion, conſents to marry him, but juſt as they are going to church, Prince Prettyman meeting, by chance, with old Joan, the handler's widow, and remembring it was ſhe that firſt brought him acquainted with Chloris, out of a high point of honour breaks oſt his match with Chloris, and marries old Joan Upon which Chloris, in deſpair, drowns herſelf, and Prince Prettyman, diſcontentedly, walks by the river-ſide This will never do 'tis juſt like the reſt. Come, let's be gone

Moſt of the Players Ay, pox on't, let's go away [*Exeunt*

Enter Bayes

Bayes A plague on them both for me, they have made me ſweat to run after 'em. A couple of ſenſeleſs raſcals, that had rather go to dinner, than ſee this play out, with a pox to 'em What comfort has a man to write for ſuch dull rogues? Come, Mr ——— a ——— where are you, Sir? Come away, quick, quick

Enter Stage keeper

Stage-k Sir, they are gone to dinner

Bayes Yes, I know the gentlemen are gone, but I aſk for the players.

Stage-k Why, an't pleaſe your worſhip, Sir, the players are gone to dinner too

Bayes How! are the players gone to dinner? 'Tis impoſſible! The players gone to dinner! i gad, if they are, I'll make 'em know what it is to injure a perſon that does 'em the honour to write for 'em, and all that A company of proud, conceited, humourous, croſs-grain'd perſons, and all that I'gad I'll make 'em the moſt contemptible, deſpicable, inconſiderable perſons, and all that, in the whole world, for this trick. I gad I'll be reveng'd on him, I'll ſell this play to the other houſe

Stage k Nay, good Sir, don't take away the book you'll diſappoint the company that comes to ſee it acted here this afternoon

Bayes That's all one, I muſt reſerve this comfort to my ſelf, my play and I ſhall go together, we will not part, indeed, Sir

Stage k But what will the town ſay, Sir?

Bayes The town! Why, what care I for the town? I'gad the town us'd me as ſcurvily as the players have done, but I'll be reveng'd on 'em too, for I'll lampoon 'em all And ſince they will not admit of my plays, they ſhall know what a ſatyriſt I am And ſo farewel to this ſtage, i gad, for ever [*Exit* Bayes.

Enter Players

1 Play. Come then, let's ſet up bills for another play

2 Play Ay, ay, we ſhall loſe nothing by this, I warrant you

1 Play I am of your opinion But, before we go, let's ſee Haynes and Shirley practiſe the laſt dance, for that may ſerve us another time

2 Play I'll call 'em in I think they are but in the tiring-room

The Dance done

1 Play Come, come, let's go away to dinner [*Exeunt Omnes.*

CPSIA information can be obtained
at www.ICGtesting.com
Printed in the USA
BVHW061400090519
547845BV00008B/918/P

9 781170 392065